campari
and soda bread

Debra Wenlock

Published by Linenopolis
101 Princetown Road,
Bangor, Co Down BT20 3TG
Northern Ireland, 2003

Designed by Gavin Walker.
Printed in Ireland by Universities Press, Belfast.
www.debrawenlock.co.uk
debra.wenlock@virgin.net

ISBN 0-9545322-0-1

Campari and soda bread

Limited Edition

This book is number 851 **of only 1000 copies**

Signed

Debra Wenlock

Debra Wenlock

To Heroes everywhere

I chose the title 'Campari and Soda Bread' to illustrate the curious mix of the exotic and the everyday – the international playboy racing drivers and the people of Ulster, the glamour of the exotic visitors mixed with the huge enthusiasm of the local population.

While these elements might seem to be in contrast, in fact they combined most successfully, and for TT week each year, between 1928 and 1936, Ulster shone at its brightest.

The world-famous superstars of racing shone too, putting on a great show both on and off the track. Sadly, many of these bright stars were to be extinguished before their time. The genial Alfa Team driver, Giuseppe Campari and many of his fellow racers including Borzacchini, Birkin, Hamilton and Seaman all died in Grand Prix racing before the end of the Thirties.

That we remember them after all this time only underlines their place in Irish, and indeed World motor-racing history.

In these paintings, I have tried to convey something of the excitement of nine annual occasions of high drama and daring. I hope this comes across. In any case, I have certainly enjoyed the journey.

Debra Wenlock

Contents

Page

Photographs

Front cover illustration; Alfa Romeos of Birkin, Campari and Howe at Glen Hill, 1931.

Rear cover illustration; detail of Austin Seven Ulster at Butcher's shop corner, 1929.

Foreword

When Debra Wenlock first arrived from England in 1987, she was met by friends including a future transport museum curator, a Cosworth development engineer and myself, a motoring hack, with a 1959 Austin Cambridge in the car park.

Since then, barely a day has gone by without cars of one vintage or another figuring largely and, given her own huge artistic talent, it was inevitable they should dominate her work. She now paints overlooking a garage housing an Austin Seven, a Fiat Topolino and a Tornado Typhoon and has completed many commissions of similarly varied machinery.

These pictures are her most ambitious so far, depicting the Ards TT Races, the heyday of road-racing, from the late 1920s to the mid-30s.

A race programme of the time gives an insight into the importance of the Ards circuit, listing some of the all-time greats such as Nuvolari, Caracciola, Sir Henry Birkin, Malcolm Campbell and of course 'Fast Freddie' Dixon. In 1929 alone, seventy-three drivers entered twenty-one different makes and represented six different countries, all pushing their machines to the limit through the narrow lanes and town streets of north Down.

It is hard now to imagine that Northern Ireland was at that time a centre for what was essentially the equivalent of today's Formula One racing.

In more than a score of paintings, Debra has set out to bring to life the Ards TT era, capturing the fearless spirit of those men, the raw speed and power of their cars and the freedom and style of an era that was about to disappear forever.

Richard Sherriff
Motoring Correspondent
Belfast News-Letter

Introduction

A total of nine Tourist Trophy races were held on the Ards course, the first being held in 1928. One of the purposes of the race was to help develop sports cars for ordinary private use. Drivers competed in cars similar to those supplied to the public and the regulations were regularly modified to remind factory teams of this. Superchargers were permitted for the first six years, but banned from 1934 onwards. The ban was unpopular with spectators who loved the wail that they made.

The race was originally thirty laps, giving a distance of four hundred and ten miles, and lasted about six hours. By 1932, the winner, CR Whitcroft, completed the distance in five hours. So in 1933 the race was increased to thirty-five laps giving a distance of four hundred and seventy-eight miles. This proved a strain on drivers and tyres without serving any real purpose, so in 1936 the race was reduced to its original distance.

1928

The first year saw a great duel between Kaye Don and Leon Cushman with only fifteen seconds between them at the start of the final lap. Don won by thirteen seconds and Cushman ran out of petrol immediately after crossing the line.

During the 1928 race, an Avro Avian aeroplane piloted by Sir Alan Cobham caused a big thrill when it had to make a forced landing in Mr McKee's field a short distance from the course at Dundonald.

1929

The second year Rudolf Caracciola's huge Mercedes hunted down the cars ahead of him. Then it began to pour with rain and everyone slowed down except Rudi 'Regenmeister' (rain master) who increased his speed. The harder it rained the faster he drove. The sound of his screaming supercharger was the signal for rapturous cheering whenever he appeared. He won, passing poor Campari on the last lap. Archie Frazer-Nash gained third place in his Austin Seven. Sadly, a crash at Ballystockart claimed the lives of driver Frank Clark and breakdown member John Kelly.

1930

Before the race, part of the course had to be resurfaced after a traction engine with studded rear tyres had driven over it causing £200 worth of damage. The driver was fined forty shillings.

It was estimated that half a million people watched the race. Rain made the roads treacherous and many skids were witnessed.

Kaye Don was saved by spectators when his car overturned, caught fire and was destroyed. Birkin's Bentley later crashed at Ballystockart.

The day ended in triumph for Italy's Alfa Romeo team when Nuvolari, Campari and Varzi, gained first, second and third places respectively.

Only half of the thirty-six starters completed the course. Special praise was given to the Talbot team who ran non-stop throughout the race.

1931

It was expected that Nuvolari would repeat his previous year's win but he retired early on with a seized engine. The MGs and Alfas fought with each other and Campari fought with everyone. The privately entered Alfas of Birkin and Howe retired. With Nuvolari out and Campari slowing, the Alfa team signalled Borzacchini to go all out for a win. He was pipped at the post by Norman Black in an MG Midget entered by the Earl of March.

1932

Great crowds were present and the weather was perfect. There were several thrilling incidents. Major Gardner crashed his MG Midget, breaking his leg, and four spectators were injured at Ballystockart when a car crashed into a garden.

Freddie Dixon, a newcomer to car racing, set an amazing pace in a Riley Nine before crashing into a rhubarb field at Quarry Corner. Tim Birkin raised the lap record to over 83mph in his Alfa.

Only ten cars out of the thirty-two starters finished the course, the first three finishers were Whitcroft (Riley), George Eyston (Riley), Eddie Hall (MG Midget).

1933

Belfast shops and businesses closed on race day – such was the enthusiasm for the race. Spectators used trams, buses, cars, motorbikes, bicycles and even jaunting-cars to reach the course.

Nuvolari gained his second Ards TT win, this time in an MG. Second place went to local man Hugh Hamilton who was only forty seconds behind after a botched pit stop lasting eight minutes that should have taken three. Third place went to Tim Rose-Richards in a supercharged Alfa.

Eyston was driving a Riley when it developed clutch trouble. By emptying a fire extinguisher into the clutch and later by adding sand, he managed to finish the race.

1934

Earl Howe had an unpleasant experience during practice when a bird shattered his Talbot's windscreen while he was driving at 80mph.

On the day of the race, only seventeen out of forty starters finished the course.
Great crowds were present and, except for some rain on the Ards straight towards the end of the race, the weather was perfect.

The feature of the day was a spectacular 100-mile dogfight between Eddie Hall's Rolls-Bentley and Brian Lewis' Lagonda.

A Riley driven by HB Prestwich ran wide at Quarry Corner, bounced into the field and landed upside down. A sigh of relief came from the crowd when the driver appeared from beneath his car and clambered up the bank, apparently unharmed but extremely muddy.

The first three finishers were CP Dodson (MG Magnette), ER Hall (Rolls-Bentley) and T Fotheringham (Aston Martin).

1935

The year was a disaster for the Singer team. Three out of the four cars entered crashed because of a steering fault. The fourth car was withdrawn immediately. Fortunately no one was seriously hurt, but the incident did Singer a great deal of harm.

It was a day of brilliant sunshine and huge crowds lined the course. The roads were in perfect order.

During the race a horse found its way on to the Dundonald sector of the course. It galloped up the road for a couple of hundred yards before being diverted into a field. Driving with rare judgement and at a consistently high speed, Freddie Dixon won the eighth Ards TT race. Eddie Hall was second and Earl Howe third.

1936

More top names returned in the final year of the Ards; Prince Bira, Dick Seaman, and the French Delahaye team. It rained heavily in the early stages of the race, but as the weather improved, so did the lap times.

Lebegue set the lap record at a time faster than the speed tables in the race programme. In mid afternoon a local driver skidded on the way into Newtownards town and struck a lamppost killing many spectators. Most people did not learn of the tragedy until they read about it in the newspapers after the race finished.

Charlie Dodson and Freddie Dixon shared their second wins at Ards. The winning car was driven over the line by Dodson with Eddie Hall coming in second for the third year in a row.

The last race of the Ards TT series was run.

From Blighty to Belfast

No fewer than fourteen vessels berthed at Donegall Quay, each of them had a full compliment of passengers. Visitors numbering many thousands, arrived by the various steam ship routes

Belfast News-Letter

Race Preparations

Immense crowds watched the practice for the TT. I was amazed at the dense throngs of onlookers all round the course. Passing through Newtownards and Comber one was almost deafened by cheering and shouts of encouragement

The Motor

Practice

All of us who crowd space into time have had hairbreadth escapes

Malcolm Campbell

Captain Birkin's Message to Ulster

To the Editor of the Belfast News-Letter

Sir – At the conclusion of my third delightful stay in Belfast I am at a loss to find words to express my admiration for the manner in which the Tourist Trophy race was organised and carried through, for the wonderful enthusiasm and sportsmanship of the Ulster people, and last but by no means least, for the astonishingly efficient manner in which the police carried out their extremely difficult task.

Ulster has nothing to fear from the competitors' point of view with regard to the race being held elsewhere, so long as it is organised as it was this year, and whilst such wonderful enthusiasm is displayed by officials and public alike.

If I may be allowed to strike one personal note, may I add how deeply I appreciated the innumerable kindnesses which were shown to me and to the Bentley team during our stay in Ulster.

Next year we will hope to see the Tourist Trophy regained for Great Britain. – Yours &c.,

Henry Birkin
166 Piccadilly, London
30th August 1930

The 'Scrutineers'

1936

The Delahayes of which so much had been expected, had wretched luck. Their much-feared challenge quickly faded out. The cars made a bad start, several suffered from minor troubles, one crashed, and two of the six retired. Delahaye No10, driven by René Lebegue, had the distinction of setting the all-time lap record at 9mins 33secs – 85.52 mph, before having to retire from the race.

The thing I remember most about the TT was the amazing noise

Spike Kennedy, small boy at the 1936 TT aged 6yrs 1 month

Motor
DIA TYRES
10

The Start

1929

The 1929 Le Mans-type start had competitors dashing across the road to flick down their hoods and away. Bentley No73 was entered by 'Babe' Woolf Barnato and driven by Glen Kidston who later crashed it on Bradshaw's Brae. A fine sportsman, Kidston led a charmed life until he died in an aeroplane crash in South Africa in 1931. He had already survived another plane crash and a submarine accident.

There were no TTs like the Ards TTs, and no Ards TT like 1929

Richard Hough - Tourist Trophy, the History of Britain's Greatest Motor Race

ON TOP IN ALL ROAD TESTS
PRATTS AT ALL EVENTS
SUPREME ON LAND AIR & WATER
ISLE OF MAN Senior T.T. Junior T.T.
ULSTER T.T. Fastest Lap
SCOTTISH SIX DAYS All Premier Awards
Pratts
KING'S CUP 1st & 2nd
SCHNEIDER TROPHY 1927
Duke of Yorke TROPHY
SIDDELEY TROPHY
Pratts
67
70
72
73
Debra Wenlock

And they're off!

1930

Bentley Boys away! No1 Captain Tim Birkin, No2 Bertie Kensington Moir, No3 Dr Dudley Benjafield, No4 Eddie Hall. Britain's chief hope in the 1930 event was placed in Birkin, but his Bentley hit a telegraph post and a wall at Ballystockart. Bertie finished 11th overall and Eddie Hall took 12th place. Dr Benjafield was flagged off after twenty-seven laps. The fuel consumption of a supercharged Bentley was around 8mpg.

There are very, very few people one can trust to drive a car at 125mph on an ordinary road

Captain Birkin referring to Bertie Moir

LAND AIR & WATER
ON TOP IN ALL ROAD TESTS
DUNLOP
Pratts MOTOR OIL
The Autocar
Debra Wenlock

The first lap

1928

Bentley No54 completed its first lap, driven by the shy and modest Humphrey Cook, in the first TT. He had crashed into a wall at Mill Corner during practice but finished seventh overall in the race. Cook became a favourite of Comber, where he was staying. The Bentleys of Birkin and Cook were prepared and stored in the coach house at Kane's yard just off the Square in the town. He went on to race for ERA.

I love this sort of thing. It's a grand course, and very sporting and I'm keen that there should be a race here next year. Everyone was very good to us

Humphrey Cook

RAC
INTERNATIONAL
TOURIST TROPHY RACE 1928.
DISTANCE ONE CIRCUIT 13.6 Mls
TOTAL DISTANCE 410 MILES
CONTINUOUS
LEADER BOARD
1st 2nd 3rd 4th 5th 6th
CLASS . F .
CLASS . F .
COACHES
FOR
DAYS TOURS
ONIBUS Co Ltd
54

In the pits

1928

Bugatti No50 in the pits. Owned and driven by Viscount Curzon (later Earl Howe), it retired with a split petrol tank after Campbell's similar car had been burnt out. Viscount Curzon had only recently taken up competition work, although his motoring career dated from the late 1890s. It was said that he had more convictions against him for speeding than any other motorist in Great Britain.

I am attracted to this great Ulster event mainly because it affords the opportunity to drive for over 400 miles without fear of police traps!

Viscount Curzon in an address to Boy Scouts helping in the race

50

Picnic at Quarry Corner

1935

The ladies are sheltering beside their AC Tourer whilst the Lagondas of Hindmarsh and Dodson race by. Admission to the enclosure at Quarry Corner was five shillings per person and ten shillings for the car. Le Mans winner, No1 John Hindmarsh led the race at one stage but tyre changes and a choked petrol line slowed him up until he eventually finished in seventh place. The previous TT winner, No2 Charlie Dodson smacked a bank at Moate before finishing eighth.

Hindmarsh tore past the pits blowing his horn and indicating with a thumb that sundry smaller fry should move over and make room

The Motor

The Wizard of Ards

1932

Freddie Dixon in his Riley, shortly before his famous leap into a field. On the 25th lap, Fast Freddie came up to Quarry Corner too fast. The car, with riding mechanic Len Ainsley, leapt over the bank into a rhubarb patch. Dixon had the presence of mind to switch off the ignition whilst in mid-air. Damage was limited to a buckled wheel, and a few cuts and bruises. After the race, Dixon changed the wheel, persuaded some spectators to push the car out of the field and drove back to the pits.

The pace was too hot, too hot even for Freddie Dixon who had set it in a madcap drive which ended with a wrecked car

Belfast News-Letter

AILY MAIL
DUNLOP
BP PLUS
DUNL
Friday
4d
Largest
Karpol
DUNLOP
20
Debra Wenlock

Cornering at Quarry

1932

Alfa Romeo No3 driven by Tim Birkin and his riding mechanic Major Humphrey Butler rounding Quarry Corner. Birkin finished in fifth place overall in this, his last, TT. He was badly burned when taking part in the Tripoli Grand Prix in May 1933. Blood poisoning set in, and despite the best possible medical attention, he succumbed in the following month.

Birkin was a sportsman to the backbone

Malcolm Campbell

3
3

LeaFy Glade

1928

Kaye Don's victory in the first Ards TT, in car No24, was the highest sporting achievement of the Lea Francis car company. In the same year, Don broke the lap record at Brooklands at a speed of 131.45mph. He is seen here leading Vernon Balls' Amilcar No6. Balls was quietly fancied to win. He completed twenty-three laps before crashing at Newtownards.

Vernon Balls skidded in Newtownards on his Amilcar. After having his head bandaged he left the local hospital and was greeted with cheers as he passed along the Newtownards streets

Belfast News-Letter

24
24
6
DebraWenlock

Alfa Allsorts

1931

Alfa Romeos, No11 Birkin, No7 Campari, No10 Howe – at Glen Hill. Howe tried to pass Campari on Bradshaw's Brae. His Alfa struck a kerb, spun, and landed in a potato field. He drove down the field, apologised to the farmer, proceeded through the farmyard and back onto the course. The damage suffered forced his retirement. While duelling with Campari, Birkin ran out of road and hit the butcher's shop in Comber. He got going again, but, was out of the running. Campari finished sixth.

Most famous of all the circuits is at the Ards, a genuine road circuit better than any on the continent. On this circuit there is practically every type of corner, and all of them extremely interesting

Earl Howe

INDIA
DUNLOP
7
11
Debra Wenlock

Bradshaw's Brae

1936

Eddie Hall completed the whole race in 1936 without stopping to refuel. A disappointed Eddie came in second for the third year in a row, one minute behind the winning Dixon/Dodson Riley. One of only two men to compete in every Ards TT race, Hall shared this distinction with Earl Howe.

A very capable driver, Hall never gives the impression of apparent recklessness that one often sees, yet he is one of the fastest drivers in Europe

Belfast News-Letter

Debra Wenlock

Bira Blue

1935

Bryan De Grineau sketches as Prince Bira of Siam, in his Aston Martin Ulster, chases Von der Becke's Riley through Conway Square. He was later forced to retire when a broken pipe poured oil onto the hot exhaust for the third time. His blue racing livery was based on a sample of fabric cut (with her permission) from a young Danish girl's evening frock.

It was always a real pleasure to go to Belfast. Circumstances would have to be very much in favour of another place before I would forgo a trip to Northern Ireland

Prince Chula of Siam

The Leading Motoring Paper
The Autocar
FOUNDED 1895
Every Friday
4D.
Largest Circulation
DUNLOP
ELECTRICITY
Electricity
CONWAY SQUARE
20
OS

Team Talbot

1932

Talbots No4, Hon. Brian Lewis and No5, Johnny Hindmarsh pass through Conway Square. The Talbot team cars were based at Agnew & Graham's garage in Belfast's Oxford Street. The drivers were surrounded by admirers from the moment they arrived off the ferry. Talbot No4, driven by Brian Lewis lost a rear wheel at Quarry Corner during practice. Lewis finished seventh in the race despite hitting Stan Barnes' spinning MG Midget at Glen Hill.

Motor Race Hints: keep your dog at home. A stray dog on the course may cause disaster

Belfast News-Letter

PHONE
M HERE
Players Please
SMOKE
Park Drive
WILL'S
GOLD
FLAKE
ANDER FILSON
DAILY MAIL
FOR MOTORING NEWS
DUN
PRATTS
AT ALL
EVENTS
5
5
4
4
Debra Wenlock

Alvis has left the Square

1928

1928 Leon Cushman's front wheel drive Alvis enters South Street, Newtownards. His initial, "C", over the headlamp was for identification by the pit crew. During the race, Cushman hit a bank and his mechanic was thrown from the car and knocked unconscious. Cushman lifted him back in, to conform with the rules, and proceeded. On the next lap the mechanic waved to the crowds to indicate that he had recovered. They finished second overall.

Step outside the pages of humdrum existence and live for a while with men who have made, of speed, a sport for their adventure-loving selves

Malcolm Campbell

32
C
Debra Wenlock

1934

Three Magnettes

MG Magnettes, No25 George Eyston, No26 Wal Handley, No27 Charlie Dodson on Comber Straight. Dodson went on to win the race at an average speed of 74.65mph, whilst Handley retired with engine trouble after seventeen laps and Eyston retired after thirty laps, also with engine trouble.

Eyston is one of speed's greatest exponents

Malcolm Campbell

26
26
25
25
27
Debra Wenlock

Fane's red face

Frazer Nash BMW, No18, driven by AFP Fane braves miserable weather, to finish third overall. Its radiator grille was painted red to distinguish him from his team mates Aldington, whose radiator was white and Prince Bira, with blue.

1936

It was decided to use my pit signals. These were Siamese characters on a coloured background, and we had much amusement in teaching Fane and Aldington to remember all those signals

Prince Chula

18
18
IIA 44983
IIA 44983
DebraWenlock

Seven at butcher's shop corner

1929

The Austin Seven of Caldicutt and Brockas has just negotiated the butcher's shop corner at Comber. It finished 19th. It was found that the standard cars could not keep up with the handicap, so superchargers were brought from the factory in England and fitted the night before the race in Harry Ferguson's Belfast garage. The other Austin Sevens finished 3rd, 4th and 16th.

When cars go astray at Comber, they usually make a bee-line for the butcher! ..... even though the butcher's shop is a danger spot, the windows are always crowded with onlookers!

Malcolm Campbell

OILS.
DISTEMPER
S.NI
3

Model A Ford in Comber

1929

Local man Stanley Wright drove in the 1929 TT in a Model A Ford. He never stood a chance of even a class win as he was up against the supercharged cars of Ettore Bugatti's works team. The Belfast and County Down Railway line shadowed the course for much of the route and ran a frequent service on race days.

Smoking and drinking should be cut down to the minimum a fortnight before the event

George Eyston- advice to racing drivers

Wines MACDONALD Spirits
MACDONALD
59

Caracciola's winning Mercedes

Rudi Caracciola's winning Mercedes on the Comber-Dundonald stretch. His team mate Otto Merz, driving No71, was disqualified for removing a mudguard from his car (with his bare hands). Merz had previously been a chauffeur in the service of Archduke Franz Ferdinand of Austria and was on duty with him when he was assassinated in Sarajevo.

1929

In some ways the value of a supercharger was more psychological than practical. This was never truer than of the Mercedes whose banshee wail boosted the driver's ego in the same proportion as it disconcerted his competitors

GN Georgano

70
70
Debra Wenlock

Frazer Nash at the hairpin

1934

Frazer Nash driven by The Hon. Peter Mitchell-Thompson leads the Singer of Alf Langley into the Dundonald hairpin. Mitchell-Thompson was a son of Lord Selsdon of Croydon, a former Postmaster General. He finished fifteenth overall. The most popular Frazer Nash model was a TT Replica. Langley managed to complete the distance in the Singer but was flagged off the course after thirty five laps for being out of time.

Motor racing is a man's game, calling for iron nerves and quick action. To those of us who practise it the starter's flag is a lovely sight and the boom of a maroon is music

George Eyston

ONALD HAIRPIN BEND
PRATTS ETHYL
The Motor
Castrol
DAILY EXPRESS
15
22
Debra Wenlock

Nuvolari at the hairpin

Tazio Nuvolari in the winning MG K3 Magnette, No17, cornering Dundonald hairpin. He broke the lap record seven times during the race and won by a mere forty seconds. Omagh man Hugh Hamilton was second.

1933

To those of us who crowd the miles into minutes, there is unalloyed bliss in the control of a racing car whose well-tuned engine is pitted against those of our racing colleagues

George Eyston

THE CENTRAL
DUNLOP
The Autocar
Every Friday
4D.
Largest
"BP"
Essolube
THE ONLY 5 STAR MOTOR OIL
WHISKEY
17
17

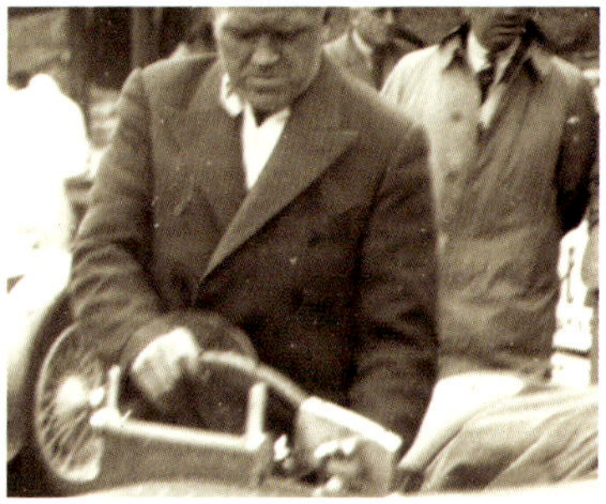

1936

The final winner

Freddie Dixon and Charlie Dodson shared the driving of the Riley which won the last Ards TT race. For both of them this was their second TT win. After the race hundreds of young boys charged their pit seeking their autographs.

I hope you all enjoyed yourselves, I know I did

Freddie Dixon

26

The Final Score

The highlights of the racing game are its successes and its escapes. I have experienced them both, and when the time comes for me to hand over the wheel to younger men I shall have a wealth of memories to comfort me; I shall have lived

George Eyston

Autographs

Bibliography

Flat Out by GET Eyston with foreword by Sir Malcolm Campbell, 1933

The Luck of the Game Again by Barré Lyndon, MG 1934

Sir Malcolm Campbell's Book of Famous Motorists by M Campbell & RS Lyons, Blackie & Sons, London 1937

Road Racing 1936 by Prince Chula of Siam, Foulis & Co, London 1946

Blue and Yellow by Prince Chula of Siam, Foulis & Co, London 1947

Three Pointed Star by David Scott Moncrieff, Cassell, London 1955

Tourist Trophy, The History of Britain's Greatest Motor Race by Richard Hough, Hutchinson, London 1957

Nuvolari by The Earl Howe, Seeley Service & Co, London 1959

The Story of the Motor Car by David Carey, Ladybird, Loughborough 1962

A History of Sports Cars by GN Georgano, Nelson Publishing 1970

The Story of the MG Sports Car by F Wilson McComb, Dent, London 1970

The Ards TT by Ulster Vintage Car Club and John Moore 1978

Winners edited by Brian Laban, Orbis Publishing, London 1981

Bentley, the Vintage Years by Michael Hay, Dalton Watson, London 1986

Motor Racing by The Earl Howe, Seeley Service & Co, London

Periodicals

Ards Chronicle

Belfast News-Letter

Northern Whig

Belfast Telegraph

Autocar

The Motor

Motorsport

The Automobile

Classic Car Mart

County Down Spectator

Classic and Sportscar

Classic Cars

Automobile Quarterly

RAC Tourist Trophy Programmes

UVCC Tourist Trophy Programmes

Acknowledgements

I am most grateful to the many individuals and organisations who have helped by sharing their cars, their memories, their photographs, their support and most importantly their enthusiasm.

This book would not have been possible without the kind assistance of Andy Anderson, Mark Kennedy, Gavin Walker, Richard Sherriff and the outstanding knowledge of local motoring historian Simon Thomas.

Ken Anderson, Ards Arts, Ards Borough Council, Ards Historical Society, Clifford, Gina & Conor Auld, The Bests, Terrence & Jenny Bradley, Gordon Buckley, Robin Cameron, George Crowe, Tom Ferris, Mary Galbraith, Guild of Motoring Artists, Rosaline Henderson, Alan & Barbara Henry, Chris Hudson, Andy & Heather Johnson, Mike Johnson, Dermot Johnson, Spike Kennedy, Roger Key, Nigel McComb, Rodney McComb, Basil McCoy, Des McDowell, Stanley McMaster, Patrick McMillen, John Moore, Terry & Ros Murphy, Leslie & Yvonne Murray, DB McNeill, Jonathan Neild, The Lord O'Neill, Maureen Paige, Billy Patterson, Mickey Phinn, The Royal Automobile Club, Paul Shields, Sally Skilling, The Smarts, Trevor Smith, Ian Titterington, Simon & Liz Thomas, Ulster Automobile Club, Ulster Folk & Transport Museum, Ulster Vintage Car Club, Chris Ward, Phil & Pat Wenlock, Mike Wilson.

And to the many others who have kept the chequered flag flying; The Lord Dunleath and Lady Dunleath, Billy Galbraith, Mike Wylie, Mawhinney's butcher's shop in Comber, The Spence Brothers, the TT Lounge in Comber.

The Prize

Racing is life.
Anything before or after is just waiting

Steve McQueen